Salmon

Salmon

A Carolrhoda Nature Watch Book

by Ron Hirschi

Carolrhoda Books, Inc. / Minneapolis

CONTENTS

The Salmon People   7
The Salmon Family   10
Birth in River Stones   16
To Sea and Back   22
Salmon in Danger   33
Salmon Savers   40
Glossary   46
Index   47

For Anne with thanks to Mike Reed

Carolrhoda Books, Inc.
A division of Lerner Publishing Group
241 First Avenue North
Minneapolis, MN 55401 U.S.A.

Website address: www.lernerbooks.com

LIBRARY OF CONGRESS CATALOGING-IN-PUBLICATION DATA

Hirschi, Ron.
    Salmon / by Ron Hirschi.
     p.   cm.
    A Carolrhoda nature watch book.
    Summary: Examines the anatomy, habitat, behavior, life cycle, and legends of the torpedo-shaped fish.
    Includes index.
    ISBN 1–57505–482–5 (lib. bdg. : alk. paper)
    1. Salmon—Juvenile literature. [1. Salmon.] I. Title. II. Series
QL638.S2 H54   2001
597.5'6—dc21   00–008382

Manufactured in the United States of America
1 2 3 4 5 6 – JR – 06 05 04 03 02 01

Left: *Sockeye salmon swim close together as they make their way upstream.*
Right: *A chinook salmon swims in the fresh water of the North Umpqua River, Oregon.*

THE SALMON PEOPLE

Salmon have graced rivers, streams, and the seas for many centuries. All salmon are born in freshwater. Most then swim to the vast Pacific Ocean. Toward the end of their lives—as if by magic—they return to the same river or stream where they were born. There, they mate and produce their own young, beginning the cycle again.

For generations, native people of the Northwest coast of North America have celebrated the return of the salmon to their rivers. Elders pass along the story of the salmon people to their children and grandchildren. The legend says salmon are people just like us. These people live far to the west on islands in the sea. Each year, the salmon people shed their clothes, sprout fins, and swim to rivers. The salmon people offer themselves to humans. The humans catch the salmon and enjoy a feast of fresh fish. They also treat the fish with great respect to ensure their return.

Sockeye salmon rest in a pool before heading upstream to spawn.

Since this legend was first told, biologists have learned much more about salmon, their **habitat** (the place where they live), and their special needs. But even with that knowledge, we seem unable to protect them from threats to their existence. Salmon face dangers from dams, logging, overfishing, and many kinds of habitat changes.

The salmon people of legend would probably not want to swim through waters full of nets, pollution, and dams. But a new kind of "salmon people" have appeared along the coast. These people are not fictional characters but real people. They work hard to protect the fish, restore salmon habitat, and help make rivers and oceans a safe home. Some of these salmon people are biologists, some are engineers, and many are kids who want to make a difference in a stream near their home.

A chinook salmon bursts through the water of Oregon's North Umpqua River.

THE SALMON FAMILY

Salmon are members of the fish family Salmonidae, which also includes trout and char. There are seven different species commonly called Pacific salmon. Their **range,** or area in which they naturally live, includes North America and northern Asia. Chinook, coho, chum, sockeye, and pink salmon are native to both sides of the Pacific. Masu and amago salmon are native only to Asia. Fishers have also introduced salmon to other locations, including the Great Lakes and New Zealand. Atlantic salmon have been introduced to the Pacific coast, but they are not discussed in this book.

All salmon are sleek, silver fish with darker, bluish green backs. Each has a deeply forked tail. Salmon **fins,** the appendages they use for swimming, are fairly soft—much softer than the stiff and spiny fins of bass, rockfish, and sunfish.

Salmon returning to the stream of their birth to spawn are often brightly colored. Shown here are sockeye *(top left),* chum *(bottom left),* pink *(top right),* coho *(center), and* chinook *(bottom right)* salmon.

Salmon and their close relatives, the trout, are not always easy to tell apart. Both salmon and trout have a soft, rubbery adipose fin. This fin is set between the dorsal fin (the high fin atop their backs) and the tail. The fleshy adipose is a key physical feature distinguishing them from many other fish.

One way to tell the difference between a trout and a salmon is to look at the tail. A trout's tail is not as deeply forked. Also, a young trout has dark speckles on its fins. The large spots on a trout's sides, called parr marks, tend to be round, while a baby salmon's parr marks are oval.

Like all fish, salmon breathe oxygen through organs called **gills**. The bright red gills are found just behind the mouth. A flaplike covering protects them. It opens and closes to let water pass through from the mouth. The gill cover is streamlined, smooth, and tight-fitting when closed, like the door of an airplane. As water flows over the gills, oxygen is drawn from the water, allowing the salmon to breathe.

The parr marks of a young trout (top) *are round, while those of a young salmon* (bottom) *are oval.*

Salmon breathe underwater by using their gills to take oxygen from the water.

A distinct line runs from just behind the gill cover to the base of the salmon's tail. This narrow tube is called the **lateral line.** Along the lateral line, tiny pores connect to nerves. This helps salmon detect vibrations in the water. The lateral line system probably helps fish identify obstacles in dark or murky water. It also helps the salmon feel the approach of a seal, shark, or other **predator,** an animal that hunts other animals.

Have you ever held a fish fresh from the water? The slime that helps it slip from your hands also helps a salmon slip and slide through the water. Silvery, see-through **scales** cover most of the salmon's body. The scales overlap tightly to form a protective, yet fragile, covering. A ring is formed on each scale each winter, when growth slows slightly. Biologists use these growth markings to determine the age of salmon.

Physical features help to identify salmon, but knowledge of their unique life histories and an understanding of habitats are the true keys to knowing salmon well. The following table will help you get to know each salmon a little better. But keep in mind that every river has its own special group of salmon. Copper River sockeye and Columbia River Spring chinook are two of the better known salmon widely identified by the river of their birth. These fish cannot be easily separated from their original homes.

SALMON OF THE PACIFIC COAST OF NORTH AMERICA

	CHINOOK (also known as tyee, king, blackmouth, and spring salmon)	COHO (also known as silver and hooknose salmon)
FRY		
ADULT		
SIZE	To almost 5 feet (1.5 m) in length and 125 pounds (68.0 kg), though adults of 20 to 30 pounds (9.1-13.6 kg) are more common.	Coho grow to over 3 feet (0.91 m) and may reach 30 pounds (13.6 kg), but adults of 10 to 15 pounds (4.5-6.8 kg) are more common.
FRESHWATER LIFE HISTORY	An ocean-going and a river life history may exist in the same stream. Sea-going chinook leave the river soon after hatching, while river chinook spend a year or more in the stream. Young chinook often overwinter near coho with slight differences in habitat needs.	Coho often spend as much as 2 years in freshwater, but some leave their stream soon after hatching and grow in estuaries. Coho fry seek protected habitats, including beaver ponds, where they can spend the winter.
APPEARANCE	Fry are very silver with prominent black spots on the back. Parr marks are oblong and about the same length above and below the lateral line. Adult salmon larger than 30 pounds (13.6 kg) are almost certainly chinooks. Smaller adults can be recognized by their black gums and blotchy spots on their back and tail.	Coho fry are the most colorful of salmon babies. A purple sheen paints their bodies and their fins are orange-red. Their anal fin is tipped with a thin, white line, a mark setting them apart from other young salmon. Adults are deep blue and silver and have a distinctive white gum line.
SPAWNING	Spawning occurs after 3 to 5 years at sea, sometimes longer. Spawning adults can be recognized by their golden sheen and dark appearance.	Adults return to spawn at age 3 or 4. As they approach spawning streams, the male's nose turns down, hooking sharply.

Note: Several trout are sometimes called salmon, but their life history is much different. Steelhead, cutthroat, rainbow, and other trout may swim into the sea from early life in freshwater. But trout usually do not die after spawning. They will swim back into the sea, a lake, or a stream where their life continues, unlike their salmon relatives. Atlantic salmon are also able to spawn a second time, one feature that makes them more closely related to trout.

CHUM	PINK	SOCKEYE
(also called dog salmon)	(also known as humpy salmon)	(also called redfish, blueback, kokanee, and silver trout)

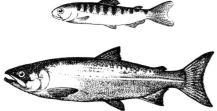

Chum are similar in size to coho, growing to about 30 pounds (13.6 kg).

Small salmon, the pinks may reach 30 inches (75 cm) and 12 pounds (5.4 kg), but a 3-5 pound (1.4-2.3 kg) adult is more common.

Sockeye usually weigh about 5 to 7 pounds (2.3-3.2 kg) but may reach 15 pounds (6.8 kg).

Chum usually go to sea soon after leaving the spawning gravel. They remain longer in the estuary, near their home stream, than other salmon. Chum also swim very close to the shore as they move to the ocean.

Like chum, pinks typically swim to sea as soon as they wiggle free of the spawning gravel.

Sockeye are unusual in many ways, especially in their use of lakes during part or all of their lives. Born in rivers, young sockeye spend 1 or 2 years in lakes before going to sea. Some sockeye are landlocked, completing their life cycle without going to sea.

Young chum are far more silvery than coho fry and have faint parr marks that do not reach below the lateral line. Chum wear no spots as juveniles or as adults.

Pink fry can be told from all other salmon by the lack of parr marks. Their slender bodies seem to glow silver and can be seen from a distance as the tiny fish swim to the sea. Adults are bright silver with large tail spots.

Young sockeye wear small, round parr marks that form mostly above, but extending slightly below, the lateral line. Adults have bright blue-green backs with fine speckling.

Chum adults return to the river at about 3 to 5 years of age. The sides of spawning chum are barred with red and dark blotches, replacing the silver sides of sea-going fish. Adult males develop the same hooked nose as coho.

Pink salmon return to the river, almost without exception, at 2 years of age. Spawning males wear a distinctive hump on their backs.

In a dramatic color change, the sides of adult sockeye turn bright red, contrasting with their greenish heads and making them one of the most photographed of all salmon.

Female (front) *and male pink salmon swim up the Sultan River, Washington State.*

BIRTH IN RIVER STONES

Born from an egg, soft and round, all salmon begin life in much the same way. Each member of the salmon family has its own particular needs, but all species have a fairly similar life history. Salmon are born in freshwater. Most salmon, but not all, **migrate,** or move, to the sea early in life. Each adult returns to the river of its birth to complete the life cycle.

Delicate salmon eggs are about the size of a pencil eraser and look like tiny red bubbles. A female carries the eggs in clusters that bulge within her body. She then **spawns,** or deposits her eggs, in a **redd,** or gravel nest.

A spawning female digs the redd with her body, scooping away small stones, silt, and sand with her belly and tail. She digs a few shallow egg pockets in the stream bottom. She will lay as many as two thousand or more eggs in the nest. Males swim nearby, trying to chase away other males. Males don't help dig the redd, but they swim near the female, nudging and swirling near her. When the time is right, a male dips over the nest and sprays his milky sperm on the eggs. The female then scoops and swishes to cover the fertilized eggs with loose stones.

Female salmon lay their eggs in a gravel nest, or redd.

The eyes of these developing sockeye salmon are clearly visible through the egg membranes. One tiny fish has hatched.

Male and female salmon complete their spawning act in the same stream where they hatched from eggs two or more years earlier. But the adults will not be present when the baby salmon wiggle free of their gravel nest. Egg and sperm production—as well as the long journey it takes to get from the ocean to the stream—greatly weakens adult salmon. The adult salmon lose as much as 95 percent of their bodies' fat reserves during migration.

The weakened females guard their nests, trying to keep others from digging a new redd on top of their own. But soon all strength vanishes. Adult salmon do not eat after entering the river. The loss of body fat and protein rapidly weakens their tissues. Both parents soon die, and their tattered bodies drift downstream, sometimes washing back into the sea.

Though without parental protection, new life is forming within the developing eggs. The growing babies are called **embryos.** The eyes are the first sign of fish growing in the eggs. The length of time it takes to develop varies greatly. Some salmon will take as little as one month to hatch, while others can take five months or even longer. In general, colder water slows the hatching process.

Once hatched, the baby salmon is known as an **alevin.** The little fish breaks free of the egg membrane, but it still wears a little pouch of egg **yolk,** like a bubble, on its belly. The egg yolk nourishes the young fish until it is able to find food on its own. Alevins are only about 1.4 inches (35 mm) long on hatching. They will swim up into the river current, but they dart down into the gravel's protection to avoid kingfishers, herons, and other predators.

Coho alevins hatch from their eggs.

Alevins gain strength as they grow and absorb the egg yolk. Still not much more than 1.8 to 2.0 inches (45–50 mm) long, the young salmon, now called **fry,** swim more freely. Fry have no parents to guide them to hiding places. Their only nest was the redd. But the little fish gather together in schools. They seek shelter and food along river edges, in rocky pools, beneath the cover of fallen logs, and even among leaves littering the streambed. Hungry trout, river otters, and many other predators catch baby salmon at this life stage.

Salmon eggs and fry are highly sensitive to stream pollution and stream habitat loss. Clean, clear water is critical for survival. The gills of the little fish absorb oxygen from the water. But oxygen is blocked when too much sand, silt, or mud washes into the stream from nearby logging or land clearing. The silt also covers hiding places in crevices between the rocks.

Coho fry

Even though pollution is a serious threat to salmon, the little fish actually need a kind of messy room within their first home. The "mess" they need includes all the leaves, sticks, and big logs that fall into the water from **watersheds,** or lands surrounding the stream. The land around most salmon streams was once covered with endless forest. In Pacific Northwest watersheds, biologists have discovered that baby salmon thrive best where old trees still line stream banks, grow to die of natural causes, then fall into the river.

Like grandparents, old trees are especially valuable. They create a shady habitat in the stream, form pools for the baby salmon, and hold stream gravel in place. When too many old trees are removed, it is as if the stream becomes unzipped, tossing aside important pieces of habitat that fish need. When kept in place, ancient trees help the baby fish as they grow and eventually move down to the sea.

In the Eagle Cap wilderness area, Oregon, dead trees have fallen into the water. The trees provide a great habitat for young salmon.

Salmon smolts swim in the estuary of Alaska's Naknek River.

TO SEA AND BACK

Young salmon ready to leave their river homes are called **smolts**. Smolts are easily recognized by their bright colors. A silver layer grows over each tiny scale, partly hiding the darker parr marks worn by younger salmon.

The smolts look like miniature versions of adult, seagoing salmon. This change helps them avoid predators like adults do. Like many ocean dwellers, the salmon are dark on the back and bright on the sides and bottom. This helps them hide from predators looking down on dark seas and from those looking up into bright, silvery light near the ocean surface.

Many smolts are swept to the sea when spring snowmelt raises water levels. Others remain in sheltered stream habitats until autumn rains swell the stream. No matter when they drift downstream, smolts enter the ocean in a special nursery ground. This area between river and sea is a place where freshwater and saltwater mix, forming an **estuary.** Within healthy estuaries you will find wetland habitats. The wetlands include marsh, eelgrass, and kelp beds. These habitats are rich feeding grounds that allow the little fish to grow rapidly.

The estuary of the Salmon River, Oregon (left), *has kelp beds* (above) *that provide rich feeding grounds for young salmon as they prepare to enter the ocean.*

23

Chum and pink salmon may be little more than 1 inch (2.5 cm) long when they arrive in the sea, so the shelter of marsh plants becomes a critical refuge. Seagoing chum hide under the cover of plants and overhanging trees along the shore. The coastal wetlands provide these little fish with a launching pad and safety net as they begin their migration to deeper seas.

Chinook smolts enter saltwater at lengths up to about 3 inches (7.6 cm). Some chinook swim into deeper waters, briefly returning to the mouth of streams and rivers where marsh habitat offers a feeding area with concentrated food sources. But their movements are poorly understood.

Salmon are not the only animals attracted to coastal wetlands. Diving seabirds, small sharks, and even whales hunt schools of salmon swimming out to sea.

As salmon grow, they move farther and farther into the Pacific Ocean. They begin to hunt new **prey,** or the animals they eat. Salmon search for small fish and shrimplike animals. As the salmon grow larger, they eat baitfish, such as herring and sandlance. These small fish begin life in shallow water, sometimes as eggs attached to kelp or eelgrass plants.

Very little is known about the life history of salmon in the open sea. This is due to the vastness of the ocean. But we do know that salmon grow quickly and that some travel far and wide before returning to their spawning rivers.

24

herring, and other small fish, including sandlance. Their appetites seem endless. Chinook measuring 10 inches (25 cm) have been observed with their mouths filled with so many baitfish that the salmon cannot close their jaws.

Young salmon continue to grow rapidly. They travel continually, moving as far as 1,000 miles (1,600 km) or more from shore. In the open ocean, fur seals, Pacific whitesided dolphins, sea lions, and humpback whales eat salmon.

As the salmon approach adult size, orca whales hunt schools of the silver-bright fish. Like wolves of the sea, the orcas hunt together. The sleek whales swim through narrow passages, hugging the shores of rocky islands, where they trap salmon against dense jungles of kelp plants.

In the river, young chinook may grow only about 1 inch (2.5 cm) in an entire year. But from April to June, chinook newly arrived in saltwater have been found to triple their length. At about 5 inches (12.5 cm) long, hungry chinook feed on crab larvae, amphipods, insects,

25

Fish predators include many other skilled hunters, like the great white and blue sharks and even other salmon. But human fishers—with their sweeping nets or their lures—catch the most salmon. Fresh salmon caught in the ocean are a prized catch for many people and an important source of income, too.

Above: *Sockeye salmon are unloaded from a fishing boat in Bristol Bay, Alaska.*
Left: *Edward Moff holds his trophy salmon. The king salmon weighed in at 95 pounds.*

Fully grown salmon leave the open ocean, turning back toward the coast. They begin a long search for the stream of their birth. As they near the shoreline, new predators greet them from above. Bald eagles dive to snatch salmon while the fish swim near the water's surface. When adult salmon make their way back through the estuary and enter the river to spawn, harbor seals, sea lions, and grizzly bears seek them out.

Both grizzlies and black bears meet spawning salmon within tidal waters—coastal shallows where seawater rises and falls with the pull of the sun and moon. The bears wade out into the river as it threads across mudflats. They also wait at waterfalls and plunge into quiet pools where the fish rest before moving farther upstream.

A salmon becomes a meal for a bald eagle.

Left: *Migrating salmon are met by a hungry obstacle.*
Below: *A salmon barely escapes the jaws of a brown bear.*

Sockeye salmon swim through shallow water to spawn in the river of their birth.

By the time salmon are within the river, the color—and even the shape—of the fish has changed dramatically. Salmon stop feeding as spawning time approaches, and their bodies lose tissue, distorting their backs and faces. Like colorful birds, the fish wear bright red and golden splashes to announce their presence, attract a mate, or warn other fish to stay away from their spawning places in the stream.

A spawning female chinook salmon digs a redd in the North Umpqua River, Oregon.

The spawning time and spawning places of each kind of salmon vary. Most salmon enter streams when river water levels are high, ensuring stream flow great enough to cover their adult-sized bodies. The largest chinook often spawn in big rivers, the females moving stones larger than your grandfather's fists as they build a redd. With the larger rocks cleared away, smaller pink salmon often nest in the same locations, placing their eggs in a shallow redd just above the eggs of the much larger chinook.

Coho with crimson red sides will spawn in the smallest of streams. The female digs with her tattered body, too often laying her eggs in streambeds that go dry when summer approaches. Some of her babies will leave the stream in spring, but many others will be trapped here, caught in a rocky channel altered by too much logging, land clearing, or other habitat changes.

Spawning coho salmon in the Soleduck River, Washington State

No matter where they spawn, adult salmon are highly visible to a growing number of new predators. Eagles continue to feast on salmon. One hundred or more bald eagles might gather along a single river to watch for the splashing, spawning fish. On the ground, raccoons join with bears. Ravens gather. Coyotes feast on fish dragged ashore by otters that are so skilled at catching the fish that they leave behind more than they can eat for themselves. Bobcats, hawks, crows, and even deer nibble at the salmon as the fish complete their life cycle.

But before the salmon are completely consumed by hungry predators, many of their bodies enter an entirely different food chain. If you walk along a salmon stream at spawning time, the fragrance of fish fills the air. To some, this is an unpleasant odor. But it is a natural reminder that the bodies of the adults are decaying. As they do, their flesh filters into the soil to nourish plants along the riverbank.

The salmon bodies also nourish the water, feeding tiny animals that are, in turn, fed upon by stream insects. Wiggling in the water, the small creatures attract the eye of hungry baby salmon. In healthy streams, the young salmon find a source of help from their now absent parents—feeding along a food chain that began when the older fish died shortly after spawning.

Above: *Dead salmon scattered along a shore provide food for bears, eagles, and other scavengers.*
Opposite page: *Salmon leap over a waterfall as they make their way upstream.*

SALMON IN DANGER

Not too many years ago, it would have seemed impossible to imagine salmon as **endangered** animals. Endangered animals are at risk of losing all members of the species forever. Fishers caught millions of pounds of salmon year after year. The harvest seemed endless to most people. But looking back, there were signs of salmon disappearance.

One way of knowing that a species is in danger is to see it vanish from some of its former places of abundance. Scientists say that a species is **extirpated** when it is gone from a specific location where it once lived. Unfortunately, salmon have been extirpated from several rivers for many years. Little by little, they vanish from even more. In many watersheds, they have reached such low population levels that it will be difficult or impossible for them to recover.

Salmon are so rare in many rivers from California to Washington State that they have been placed on endangered and threatened species lists. This means they are in danger of becoming **extinct,** or gone forever from all their former places of abundance.

Dams such as the Bonneville Dam on the Columbia River Gorge have blocked the path of many migrating salmon.

Dams are built to produce electricity or to store water for irrigation and other purposes. They also block salmon migration. They have long been one of the most severe problems facing the fish. The most devastating are the enormous hydroelectric dams on the Snake and Columbia Rivers. This vast watershed once produced as many as 20 million salmon each year.

Before dam construction, nearly half of all Columbia and Snake River fish were born in streams as far from the sea as the state of Idaho. More than one hundred dams have been built on the two rivers, and fewer than 1 of every 10 salmon born in Idaho manage to return to this watershed. Commercial fishers on the Columbia once caught enough salmon to feed people around the world. For every one hundred salmon that used to swim from the Pacific Ocean to the Columbia River, only about five complete the journey.

Dams block adult fish trying to swim upstream to spawn. The weakened adults have difficulties in natural streams, leaping waterfalls and pushing their way up rapids on their way to spawning grounds, but dams make the trip even harder. Dam builders construct fish ladders (a series of water steps built alongside the dam), but salmon use up valuable, limited energy fighting their way over these unnatural barriers.

Fish ladders have been constructed in an attempt to help salmon cross over dams.

Dams also kill many young salmon. Dams don't always prevent fish from swimming downstream, but young fish of some species, such as coho and chinook, often need to swim upstream to seek sheltered habitats or overwintering areas. The tiny fish are not strong enough to swim up and over dams because they are too weak to navigate fish ladders built with adult fish in mind. Other young salmon are simply chopped up in the dams' turbines, which are designed to produce electricity, not to allow fish to swim past.

Unfortunately, some dams completely block salmon, leading to losses of entire populations in several streams. These losses include sockeye salmon that were once able to swim up the Elwha River in Washington State. The Salmon are blocked forever by small but lethal dams on that otherwise wild and healthy river.

Habitat destruction along rivers affects almost every stream in some way. Logging, land clearing, and road construction cause erosion. Without tree roots and dense forest plants to hold it in place, soil washes into salmon streams. This leads to loss of spawning habitat when the silt fills spaces between stones in the salmon redds. The hiding places baby salmon need are also lost as silt fills the crevices they need for escape from predators.

Young salmon swim in the safety of a stream's rocky bottom.

As streamside trees are cut down, water temperatures rise, and overall water quality declines. This can be deadly to baby salmon since they are adapted to cool, clean waters. Many biologists point out the importance of water quality, knowing that many species, including humans, share many of the same needs as salmon.

Extensive habitat loss has taken place in the estuaries where young salmon need protection in their first months at sea. Salmon habitats near the shore have vanished from much of San Francisco Bay and Puget Sound. One example with a sad history is the marsh at the mouth of the Duwamish River in Seattle.

The Duwamish River is named after the people who have lived there for centuries. One of their great leaders was Chief Seattle. Seattle and his Duwamish and Suquamish tribal members were fishing for salmon at the river's mouth when the first non-Indian settlers arrived from the eastern United States. At that time, salmon were so plentiful that food supplies were not a problem, and the settlers were asked to join in the salmon feast.

Most of the trees have been removed from this area in Washington State's Cascade Mountains. Extensive logging has devastated salmon habitat.

Chinook salmon developing at the Irongate Fish Hatchery, Hornbrook, California

Since that time, docks, factories, and cargo terminals have eliminated virtually all of the marshland in the Duwamish estuary. Pollutants from the industrial area at the river's mouth also contaminate fish. This causes still more problems for the salmon and for those who eat the fish, including orca whales and people.

At one time, people thought they could have more salmon if they hatched them in captivity, then released the young fish into the sea. Surprisingly, losses often result from the creation of these salmon hatcheries. This is due in part to mass production of fish in hatcheries, using only a few parents to produce lots of young fish. In the wild, baby salmon hatch from many different parents. Each salmon has a different life history. This includes differences such as where it spends winter, what section of a stream is used for spawning, and when is the best time to swim to the sea. You see, no two salmon are alike, just like people.

Another problem with salmon hatcheries is the large number of hatchery salmon dumped into streams. Hatchery fish are often larger than their wild-born relatives, so they can displace the wild fish. Still more wild fish are lost when large numbers of hatchery fish return to the river. Scooping up nets full of the mass produced hatchery fish, fishers can and do wipe out smaller runs of wild fish returning to the same or nearby streams.

Biologists look very closely at the hatchery problem. They have found that the return of fish in rivers like the Columbia does not grow with the presence of hatcheries. Instead, the opposite is often true. More and more biologists urge the protection and restoration of wild fish adapted to wild stream conditions.

Another problem for salmon is the battle to control changes in the land, the river, and the seashore. In 1996 there were more than seven thousand applications filed in Washington State alone to make land use changes affecting salmon. These include clearing land along streams and the construction of bridges, roads, docks, bulkheads, and other structures altering stream or seaside habitats.

In most cases, permission is needed to make these kinds of land changes. But few people are available to look closely at each application. Many changes simply take place with no thought for the salmon's needs.

Chinook fry are dwarfed by a hatchery worker's feet.

A biologist examines salmon killed by toxic chemicals spilled into the Duwamish River, Washington State.

SALMON SAVERS

Biologists tell us entire watersheds must be protected and restored if we are to have salmon in the future. A watershed includes all the land from which water flows into a river or stream. Some watersheds are not much bigger than a schoolyard, sloping into a small stream that may support a few chum salmon. Others are vast. The largest North American salmon watershed outside Alaska is formed by the Columbia and Snake Rivers. It covers parts of the states of Washington, Oregon, Idaho, Montana, and Wyoming and the Canadian province of British Columbia. More than 12,000 miles (19,000 km) of streams flow in to the two major rivers, as well as tributaries including the Wenatchee, Yakima, Deschutes, Clearwater, and Willamette Rivers.

Wild salmon smolts are captured and carried around dams in containers. Despite these efforts to help the fish, many die because of the changes dams have made to their habitat.

Dam removal is the major effort proposed to restore the Columbia and Snake watershed. But that effort is caught up in political battles within the U.S. Congress. Some people argue that dams are needed to protect the local agricultural economy. Others ask that rivers be used for many purposes, including the natural support of fish and other wildlife.

Dams built by beavers create rather than destroy salmon habitat.

Removing dams is a big job. Still larger are the jobs needed to solve many other problems along the Columbia and other rivers and streams. To begin this restoration of salmon and their habitat, fishers, biologists, loggers, and interested community members have formed salmon saving groups. Go to the Internet and enter the word "salmon." You will find endless examples of environmental organizations and efforts, as well as information about salmon biology and conservation. Often fishing groups, including Northwest Indian tribes, lead these salmon saving efforts. Some schools adopt a local stream and work to protect stream banks, monitor fish populations, and restore the health of their watershed.

Ambitious efforts are also underway to restore coastal wetlands. This includes moving stream channels back to their original paths—often after highway or other construction diverted the natural flow. Often people must look at old photographs to learn where the streams and marshes were years ago.

Washington State employs loggers to place big logs in streams to restore habitats for young salmon and spawning adults. These are often the same people who cut the original stream bank trees. They are also people who call for more protection of streams—after they have learned the hard way about earlier damage done to salmon habitats.

Small hatcheries, when used wisely, can also help salmon. They are designed to bring fish back to depleted streams. The hatcheries use eggs from the same stream, or one nearby, raise and release the fish, then stop operating as soon as a healthy number of adult fish return. They don't continue to operate since the goal is to restore the stream's wild populations, not to produce unnatural hatchery populations.

The Salmon Team at Seabeck Elementary School in Seabeck, Washington, is studying and restoring the local salmon stream. Here, members of the Salmon Team, along with parents and other community members, catch young salmon and trout. The fish will be identified, measured, and counted, then returned to the stream unharmed.

Children watch salmon passing by windows at a dam on the Columbia River.

Salmon savers face many obstacles. Supermarkets, parking lots, office buildings, homes, schools, and docks along the shoreline all pose problems for fish. Even where streams are healthy, small "dams" exist at virtually every place where streams pass under highways. Culverts placed under the roadways are usually designed to allow water to pass, not fish. Many efforts are underway to replace or correct these outdated fish barriers.

Many people want to plant salmon in streams, often without knowledge of existing salmon populations or important salmon life history information. People also like to plant trees along stream banks. But sometimes the easiest thing to do, and often the best, is to protect the undamaged habitat remaining along the streams. It is important to make sure more salmon habitats are not destroyed.

Salmon savers come in all ages and sizes, and with lots of ideas. Many salmon savers have begun monitoring the different methods people have used to help fish. They net young salmon, count them, then return them to the stream to discover which method works best. They also try to understand life history information about the fish in their stream. Others monitor water quality, hoping to see high levels of oxygen, cool water temperatures, and healthy populations of stream insects.

Many people regard salmon as part of a great circle that must be continued. To make sure salmon are always with us, we must protect the path of their journey. That, in turn, will ensure the survival of these valuable fish as well as the ceremonies, stories, songs, and fun fishing times that are all part of what the salmon mean.

While salmon are in danger, many people still enjoy catching them. These happy fishers won bikes in a salmon fishing derby in Port Townsend, Washington.

GLOSSARY

alevin: a newly hatched salmon still wearing a yolk sac

embryos: animals in the early stages of development, before birth or hatching

endangered: at risk of losing all members of a type of plant or animal forever

estuary: the wide part of a river where freshwater meets and mixes with seawater

extinct: having no members of a species left alive

extirpated: gone from a specific location. Salmon have been extirpated from several rivers where they once lived.

fins: fanlike parts that stick out from the body of a fish. Fins help the fish to swim and to balance in the water.

fry: young salmon that have absorbed their yolk sac and must hunt for food

gills: organs used by fish to breathe underwater

habitat: the kind of environment in which a species normally lives

lateral line: an organ along the side of a fish that senses vibrations in the water

migrate: to move to a new area for a specific purpose, such as feeding or mating

predator: an animal that hunts other animals

prey: animals that are eaten by other animals

range: the geographic area in which a plant or animal lives

redd: a salmon's nest

scales: thin, flat plates that cover and protect fish

smolts: young salmon just going to sea, usually recognized by their bright silver color

spawns: mates, or produces young

watershed: an area of land from which water drains into a particular river or stream

yolk: nutrients stored in eggs to nourish baby salmon as they develop

INDEX

amago salmon, 10
appearance, 10–12, 14–15, 22, 29, 31
Atlantic salmon, 10

baby salmon, 18–21, 31–32, 36–37
beaver, 42
breathing, 12, 13, 20

chinook salmon, 7, 9, 10, 11, 13, 14, 24–25, 30, 36, 38, 39
chum salmon, 10, 15, 24
coho salmon, 10, 11, 14, 19, 20, 31, 36

dams, 8, 9, 34–36, 42, 44; removing, 41–42
diet, 23, 24, 25, 32

eggs, 16, 20, 30–31
erosion, 36
estuaries, 23, 27, 37

fins, 10, 12
fishing for salmon, 7, 8, 26, 33, 35, 37, 38, 45
fish ladders, 35–36

gills, 12, 13, 20

habitat, 8, 21, 23, 24, 39; loss, 8, 20, 31, 36–37, 39, 43; restoring, 9, 39, 40–45. *See also* estuaries; watersheds; wetlands
hatcheries, 38–39, 43
hiding places, 20, 21, 22, 24, 36
hunting, 23, 24, 25, 32

lateral line, 13
legends, 7–8
life span, 14–15
logging, 8, 20, 31, 36, 37

masu salmon, 10
mating, 7, 16–18, 29
migration, 7, 16, 18, 22–32; blocking, 34–36

Native American, 7, 37, 42

parr marks, 12, 14–15, 22
people and salmon, 33–45
pink salmon, 10, 11, 15, 16, 24, 30
pollution, 9, 20, 21, 37
predators, 13, 19, 20, 22, 25–28, 32, 36, 38
protecting salmon, 8–9, 39, 40–45

range of salmon, 10
redds, 16–17, 30–31, 36

scales, 13, 22
size, 14–15, 24, 25, 30
smolts, 22–24, 41
sockeye salmon, 6, 8, 10, 13, 15, 18, 26, 29, 36
spawning, 8, 14–18, 27, 29–32

tail, 10, 12
threats to salmon. *See* dams; erosion; fishing for salmon; habitat loss; hatcheries; logging; people and salmon; pollution; predators
trout, 10, 12

water quality, 37–38, 45
watersheds, 21, 33, 34, 40–41, 42
wetlands, 23, 24, 42

ABOUT THE AUTHOR

Ron Hirschi is a fisheries biologist working on salmon restoration in the Pacific Northwest. He has worked for the Washington Department of Fish and Wildlife and more recently with the Point No Point Treaty Council on salmon habitat protection.

He also spends a great deal of time working with kids and communities to restore their local watersheds, as he is pictured here (on the right, holding the net). But the truth is, he spends even more time fishing, watching fish, and dreaming of fish. His major goal in life is to catch a salmon as large as those caught by his wife, Brenda.

Ron lives on Marrowstone Island with Brenda, two labradors, and one gray cat.

PHOTO ACKNOWLEDGEMENTS

The images in this book are reproduced through the courtesy of: © Richard T. Grost, pp. 2, 7, 9, 10 (bottom), 11 (middle and bottom), 12, 16, 30, 31; © Tom Walker/Visuals Unlimited, pp. 4–5; © Natalie B. Fobes, pp. 6, 8, 10 (top), 19, 22, 26 (right), 27, 28 (right), 29, 37, 39, 40, 41, 42, 44; © Glenn Oliver/ Visuals Unlimited, pp. 11 (top), 13, 17, 20; © Kevin and Betty Collins/Visuals Unlimited, p. 18; © Bruce Berg/Visuals Unlimited, p. 21; © Martin G. Miller/Visuals Unlimited, p. 23 (left); © Hal Beral/Visuals Unlimited, p. 23 (right); © Brandon D. Cole/Corbis, pp. 24–25; Moff Family, p. 26 (left); © Nada Pecnik/Visuals Unlimited, pp. 28 (left), 33; © Patrick J. Endres/Visuals Unlimited, p. 32; © Joe McDonald/Visuals Unlimited, p. 34; © John D. Cunningham/Visuals Unlimited, p. 35; © Science VU/Visuals Unlimited, p. 36; © Mark E. Gibson/Visuals Unlimited, p. 38; © Jerry Zumdieck, p. 43; Port Townsend Leader/Miranda Bryant, p. 45.

Front cover: © Thomas Kitchin/Tom Stack and Associates
Back cover: © Thomas Kitchin/Tom Stack and Associates